ACTION SPORTS
SURFING

Joe Herran and Ron Thomas

CHELSEA HOUSE
PUBLISHERS
A Haights Cross Communications Company
Philadelphia

Chelsea House Publishers
1974 Sproul Road, Suite 400
Broomall, PA 19008-0914

The Chelsea House world wide web address is www.chelseahouse.com

Library of Congress Cataloging-in-Publication Data

Herran, Joe.
    Surfing / Joe Herran and Ron Thomas.
    p. cm. — (Action sports)

    Includes index.
    Contents: What is surfing? — Surfing gear — How a surfboard is made — Surfing safely — Skills, tricks, and techniques — Bodyboarding — Bodysurfing — In competition — Women and surfing — Surfing champions — Then and now — Related action sports.
    ISBN 0-7910-7538-9
    1. Surfing—Juvenile literature. [1. Surfing.] I. Thomas, Ron, 1947–
    II. Title. III. Series: Action sports (Chelsea House Publishers)
    GV840.S8H47 2004
    797.3'2—dc21

                                                                                    2003001184

First published in 2003 by
MACMILLAN EDUCATION AUSTRALIA PTY LTD
627 Chapel Street, South Yarra, Australia, 3141

Associated companies and representatives throughout the world.

Copyright © Joe Herran and Ron Thomas 2003
Copyright in photographs © individual photographers as credited

Edited by Renée Otmar, Otmar Miller Consultancy Pty Ltd, Melbourne
Text and cover design by Karen Young
Map by Nives Porcellato and Andy Craig
Page layout by Raul Diche
Photo research by Legend Images

Printed in China

Acknowledgements

The author and the publisher are grateful to the following for permission to reproduce copyright materials:

Cover photograph: Mark Occhilupo surfs in round two of the Billabong Pro at Teahupoo in Tahiti, May 12, 2001, courtesy of Reuters.

Getty Images, pp. 4, 13 (bottom), 18, 28, 29 (left), 30; Legend Images, pp. 5 (top), 29 (right); Reuters, pp. 13 (top), 15 (bottom), 19 (top), 23 (top), 24, 25, 26, 27; Steve Ryan, pp. 5 (bottom), 6, 7, 8, 9, 10, 11, 12, 14, 15 (top), 16, 17, 19 (bottom), 20, 21, 22.

While every care has been taken to trace and acknowledge copyright, the publisher tenders their apologies for any accidental infringement where copyright has proved untraceable. Where the attempt has been unsuccessful, the publisher welcomes information that would redress the situation.

CONTENTS

INTRODUCTION

In this book you will read about:

- surfboards and how they are made
- the gear used by surfers
- safety measures used to keep surfers safe
- the basic skills, tricks and techniques of surfing
- some of the top surfers in competition today
- the history of surfing from its beginnings in the 1700s.

In the beginning

When Captain Cook visited the Hawaiian Islands in the 1700s, he recorded that the islanders rode the waves and played in the surf. In the 1800s, going to the beach became a popular outing for people who enjoyed swimming. Most, however, were afraid to go far out into the surf.

In the early 1900s, surfing was introduced to Australia and the United States by the most famous surfer of the times, Duke Kahanamoku. He was a champion swimmer from Hawaii who won gold medals at the 1912 and 1920 Olympic Games. In 1915, Duke made tours to Australia and the United States, giving surfboard-riding exhibitions.

Surfing today

Today, surfing is a popular beach activity. There are international surfing competitions including the World Championship Tour run by the Association of Surfing Professionals (ASP).

↗ Duke Kahanamoku from Hawaii gave the first surfboard-riding demonstrations in Australia, using a board he cut from a tree after arriving.

Warning This is not a how-to book for aspiring surfers. It is intended as an introduction to the exciting world of surfing, and a look at where the sport has come from and where it is heading.

WHAT IS SURFING?

Surfing is the skill of riding waves, standing or lying down. This is usually done on a surfboard, but can also be done on a kneeboard, bodyboard, **boogie board** or inflatable mat, or using just the body.

There are four main surfing styles:

- surfboard riding is the most common form of surfing
- kneeboarding is riding while kneeling on a short surfboard
- bodyboarding is when a surfer lies flat or in a half-kneeling position on a short, foam-core board known as a boogie board
- bodysurfing is riding a wave without any equipment at all, using only the body.

↗ Surf beaches like this one are found in many parts of the world.

Where to surf?

The best beach for learning to surf is one where a sandy beach slopes gently and smoothly out into the water and where waves break softly and roll toward the shore. Beaches where there are rocks are not safe even if the surf is good.

↙ Thousands of people turn out to watch surfing competitions.

Who enjoys surfing?

Learning to surf well takes time and practice, but it is one of the most popular beach activities enjoyed by male and female surfers of all ages who enjoy the fun and exercise. There are professional surfers too, whose job it is to travel from country to country to compete in surfing competitions. One such competition is the World Championship Tour, which begins in Australia in March and moves around the world until December, when it ends in the place where surfing originated, Hawaii.

SURFING
GEAR

The surfboard

Surfboards can be long or short. A board about 10 feet (3 meters) long with a single fin is best for a beginning or inexperienced surfer. It will be steadier, more easily paddled and catch waves more quickly than a short board. Experienced surfers use shorter, narrower boards, which are easier to turn.

Nose

The nose is the front of the board. The wider the nose, the better the board catches the waves. The nose curves up to stick out of the water. This curve is called nose lift.

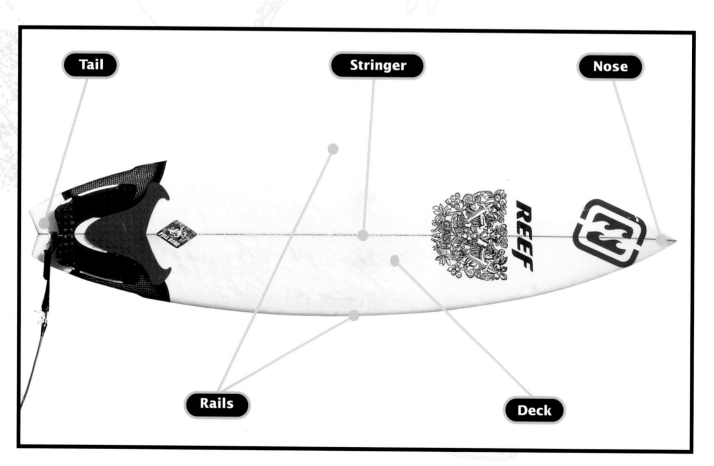

Tail   Stringer   Nose

Rails   Deck

Tail

The tail is the rear of the board. The tail curves up at the end of the board and is called tail lift.

Stringer

The stringer is a wooden piece running down the middle of the board for added strength. The length of the surfboard is the distance along the stringer, from the nose to the tail.

Rails

The rails are the sides of the surfboard. Thick rails are easier to control but thin, hard rails turn quicker.

Vee

The vee is the raised center of the bottom of the surfboard, which slopes away to the rails. This shape lets the surfer move the board from side to side and helps with turning.

Deck

The deck is the top of the board on which the surfer stands.

Fins

Surfboards can have one, two or three fins, called skegs by surfers. Fins affect the speed and flexibility of a board.

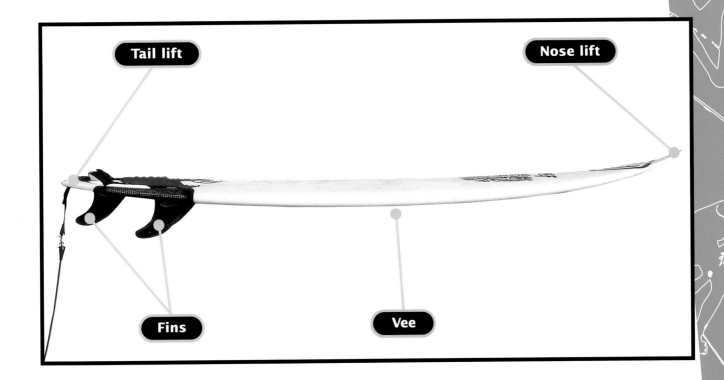

Tail lift · Nose lift · Fins · Vee

Other gear

Wetsuit

A surfer wears a stretchy rubber wetsuit to keep warm and to provide protection from cuts and abrasions from rocks, coral and other boards. A wetsuit protects the surfer from the harmful effects of the sun and keeps them warm in winter. It also helps the surfer to float. A wetsuit should be comfortable to wear and allow for plenty of movement.

Hood, helmet, gloves and boots

In places where the water is very cold, surfers wear hoods, gloves and boots to keep out the cold.

Many surfers also wear a helmet for protection from coral reefs and other surfboards.

◤ Wetsuits are lightweight and come in different styles.

Leg cords (or ropes)

Leg cords are shock-absorbing lines attached to the rear of the surfboard and fastened to the surfer's ankle with a padded **velcro** cuff. A leg cord stops the board and rider becoming separated in a **wipe-out** and saves the surfer from having to swim after the board. The rope also protects other surfers from runaway surfboards.

Wax or deck grips

Water makes the deck slippery and hard to stand on, so it is necessary for a surfer to give the deck an anti-slip surface. One way to make a sticky, rough surface is to rub **wax** onto the deck. Another method is to stick strips of textured material to the deck with waterproof adhesive. These strips are called deck grips.

↗ Leg cords are attached to the surfer's back foot.

↘ **ACTION FACT**

Surfers use different waxes on their surfboards, depending on the temperature of the water. Waxes are made for use in cold, cool or warm tropical water.

↖ Surfers rub wax onto their boards before they go into the surf to make them less slippery.

HOW A SURFBOARD IS
MADE

Although there are long and short, thick and thin surfboards with different shaped noses and tails, most boards are constructed in the same way. The foam center of the board is made of **polyurethane** or **polystyrene**. After the foam center is shaped, it is covered with layers of **fiberglass**, a woven glass cloth, and a **resin** made of **polyester**. This process is called laminating. The fin plugs are then put in. The final step in the manufacturing of a surfboard is finishing. The laminated surface is sanded to make it smooth.

During lamination, a polyester resin is pasted over the woven glass cloth.

Taking care of the board

Dents will appear in a surfboard if it is bumped. White patterns in the fiberglass, known as shatters, also appear after a board is bumped or dropped. These dents and shatters do not need to be repaired, but a broken surface will let in water and the fiberglass will lift away from the board's foam core. The foam core will become waterlogged and affect the way the board floats. Broken surfaces, called dings, must be repaired. A plastic, fiberglass resin is used to fill a broken surface, and the board is set to dry in the sun. When it is dry, the resin can be sanded for a smooth finish. Plastic putty pressed into the surface break is used for quick repairs of small dings.

Avoiding damage to the board

To avoid damage to a surfboard, the surfer:

- lies the board down flat or on its side when not in use, so that it will not fall
- does not tie a board too tightly to a car roof rack
- waxes the board on clean sand that is free of rocks and pieces of glass
- uses a cloth board cover to protect it from the sun and to keep wax off the bottom of the board.

↗ Dings, which are tears and cracks in the surfboard, must be repaired to avoid water coming into the core of the board.

SURFING
SAFELY

Surfing is a fun sport, but it can be very dangerous. To stay safe, surfers make sure they:

- are good swimmers
- never surf alone
- obey warning flags and do not swim outside the flags
- learn how to fall safely
- check out the weather conditions and watch for dangerous changes
- obey the rules of surfing.

Obeying the rules

Surfers should follow these basic rules to keep themselves and others safe and injury-free:

- when surfers are paddling for the same wave, they always give way to the surfer closest to the breaking part of the wave
- surfers do not **drop in** on another surfer's wave
- a surfer riding the wave has right of way; those paddling out try to stay out of the way.

Surfers take turns on a wave and avoid getting in each other's way.

Surfing tips

Surfers need to:

- protect their skin from the sun's dangerous ultraviolet rays by wearing vests, board shorts or wetsuits, as well as using water-resistant sunscreen
- protect their eyes from wind, sand, salt and sun by wearing sunglasses at the beach and rinsing their eyes in fresh water after they have been surfing
- protect their ears from the effects of cold water by wearing ear plugs
- wear wetsuits that trap warm air close to the body and help to keep them warm
- be aware of dangers in the water, such as sharks and jellyfish.

ACTION FACT

Hypothermia is an extreme loss of body heat that occurs when a person gets too cold. The person becomes tired, lacks the energy to keep moving, and may collapse.

↗ This surfer has been attacked by a shark. Surfers need to be alert at all times to the dangers of attack by shark.

↗ A jellyfish's tentacles are covered with venomous stingers. Surfers need to watch out for jellyfish.

SKILLS, TRICKS AND
TECHNIQUES

The basics

Surfing is a tough sport and surfers need to be fit. Exercises such as bicycle riding and running will increase the strength and stamina needed for a surfer to stay in the water for longer periods of time. Exercise will reduce the risk of injury.

Warming up

All surfers need to warm up before taking to the water. They should spend a few minutes stretching to warm up the main muscle groups in the legs and back, arms, wrists and shoulders. Walking and jogging in the sand dunes for a few minutes will get the blood circulating and warm the muscles. Warm, relaxed muscles are less likely to cramp in the cold water.

Getting into the water

The first thing a surfer learns is to walk into the surf, carrying the surfboard so that it is pointing toward the incoming waves. Once out where the waves are breaking, the surfer points the board toward the beach and shoves it forward just before a wave reaches them, then jumps onto the board and lies flat. The board catches the wave and whizzes toward the beach. As the board approaches the beach, the surfer slides off the board and into the water, at the same time pushing the board toward the beach.

When entering the water, the surfer points the nose of the board toward the surf. A sideways board can get caught by a passing wave.

Paddling out

More experienced surfers paddle out to the breaking waves. The surfer carries the board to where the water is waist deep, with the nose facing out to sea and the fins facing the body. The surfer sets the board, deck up, on top of the water. The surfer jumps to lie flat on the board and paddles out, using overarm strokes like a swimmer.

Beyond the basics

Standing up

When lying on the surfboard, the surfer grabs the rails of the board and pushes up so that the front part of the body rises off the board. Then the surfer jerks the legs up and under the body with knees bent, and stands up.

↗ For a successful ride, the nose of the board lies just above the water.

There are two ways of standing on a surfboard. Surfers who stand with their left foot in front and their right foot at the back are standing regular foot. Surfers who stand with their right foot in front and their left foot at the back are standing goofy foot.

↗ The surfer stands on the board in whichever way feels best. This surfer is standing regular foot.

Wipe-out! Learning to fall

To fall safely off the surfboard, the surfer should try to jump away from the board or push the board away so that the board does not hit her. The surfer should relax and try not to panic so that she does not become short of breath. As the surfer comes to the surface, she should protect the head and face with the arms.

In a wipe-out, the surfer tries to relax and jumps away from the board.

Riding the waves

Taking off

A surfer ready to ride a wave paddles hard to get the board moving. As the board starts to catch the wave, the surfer pushes down on the deck and swings the feet up underneath the body to stand on the board. The knees are bent and the arms are spread for balance.

> The best time to stand up is just as the board begins to drop down the face of the wave.

Turning

To keep riding along the top of a wave, the surfer needs to turn his body to the side ahead of the white water.

- **Frontside turn**

  The surfer puts weight on the back foot, leans forward over the toes of the back foot to face the wave and twists the body in the direction of the turn. When the turn is complete, the weight is shifted back to the center of the board. The arms are used for balance.

- **Backside turn**

  The surfer puts weight on the rear foot and leans back onto the heel to face away from the wave. The body is twisted in the direction of the turn and the arms are used for balance.

Turns should be quick, smooth and graceful.

Tube riding, or "shooting the tube"

The tube is a tunnel of water produced by a powerful, well-shaped wave. A tube ride is when a surfer rides inside the tunnel of water. Inside the tube the surfer bends the knees to get down low and then shifts weight to either rail as the tube changes shape and shuts down. The aim is to get into the tube and come out again without being wiped out. This is known as "being tubed".

Surfing aerials

When performing aerial tricks, the surfer flies into the air off the back of a wave, then travels some distance in the air before landing back on the board and continuing to ride it. The ollie is the basic aerial trick, named after Alan "Ollie" Gelfand, who invented the trick for skateboarders in the mid-1970s. As the surfboard hits bumps in the water caused by cross-currents, the surfer shifts weight to the back foot so that the nose lifts into the air and the board becomes airborne for a while. The surfer's knees and ankles are flexed and weight is placed on the front foot for the landing.

↗ "Shooting the tube" is an exciting but dangerous trick.

↙ Many surfing aerials are tricks that come from skateboarding.

BODYBOARDING

Bodyboards, also known as boogie boards, are made of fiberglass with a plastic foam core. They are about 3.5 feet (106 centimeters) long and 1.7 feet (52 centimeters) wide. The height and weight of the rider, as well as the rider's experience, should be considered when selecting a bodyboard. Smaller boards are easier to control, but larger boards float better and **plane** easier for a faster ride. A rider must also choose a board with a thickness that is comfortable to grip. Skegs, like fins on a surfboard, can be added to a bodyboard to help turn the board.

Bodyboarders wear a wetsuit and swim fins (flippers). Leg ropes attach the swim fins to the surfer's ankles. A leash with a cuff at one end attaches the board to the surfer's body.

Basic positions

There are two basic bodyboarding positions:

- the prone (lying) position, where the bodyboarder lies flat on the board
- the dropknee stance, where the bodyboarder half-kneels with the front foot and the back knee on the board.

A bodyboarder walks or paddles out to just past the place where the surf is breaking, and then paddles and kicks to catch a wave. Once on the wave, the surfer stops paddling and lies on the board holding the front or the rail. By shifting the body from one side of the board to the other, the bodyboarder can steer the board in the direction of the fastest ride.

Arm strap

Wetsuit

Board

Swim fins

BODYSURFING

Bodysurfing is riding waves without any equipment. In cold conditions, bodysurfers wear wetsuits. The best waves for bodysurfing are those that break before reaching the shore. **Shorebreak** waves can be dangerous and may throw a surfer into the sand.

To catch a wave, a bodysurfer pushes off from the bottom or swims toward the shore until the wave begins to lift him. Paddling a little will help the surfer to hold position on the wave. The surfer should try to keep the arms out in front of the body, to protect the head and neck. As the wave approaches the beach, the surfer turns right or left to avoid being thrown headfirst into the sand.

ACTION FACT

Some bodysurfers are now wearing soft, five-fingered gloves that are insulated. They support the palms and absorb bumps while riding the waves.

Bodysurfers wear wetsuits in cold conditions.

IN COMPETITION

Many surfing competitions are held each year. Local beaches run competitions during the summer months, and state and national competitions are held in many countries. The largest professional group of surfers is the Association of Surfing Professionals (ASP). ASP organizes events around the world for the best male and female surfers, as well as events for junior and master (older) surfers.

The World Championship Tour (WCT) is a tour for the world's top surfers. The competition begins in Australia in March and competitors travel to countries around the world. The women's competition ends in October and the men's competition ends in December—both in Hawaii, the home of surfing.

Basic rules

There are basic rules for all competitors. Two to four surfers compete in heats which last up to 30 minutes. Competitors have to catch a number of rides during the heat. A panel of five judges awards points to each surfer for:

- how well the surfer performs tricks while on the wave, and the speed and power of the performance
- how close the surfer gets to the curl of the wave when performing tricks
- choosing the best and biggest waves
- performance of tricks on all parts of the wave.

During the heat, surfers must not drop in on another surfer's wave. Any surfer who interferes with the ride of another surfer loses points.

Top surfers compete for prize money in competition at Bells Beach in Victoria, Australia.

ACTION FACT

It is important for the organizers of a surfing competition to get a complete weather forecast, and to be sure that the proper types of waves will be available for the surfers on each day of competition.

The best surfing beaches in the world

Competitions are held at beaches with world-class surf. Some of the best surf in the world is found on the ocean beaches in Hawaii. The waves travel thousands of miles across the Pacific Ocean to reach Hawaii. There, they pile up to form massive peaks many feet high before crashing forward as breaking waves.

Australia also receives some excellent surf from the Pacific Ocean, at famous beaches such as Cronulla in New South Wales. Other places with world-class surf beaches include Tahiti, Fiji, Brazil, Bali in Indonesia, California in the United States and South Africa.

↗ Giant waves known as "Jaws" rise to between 40 and 60 feet (12 and 18 meters) in height in Hawaii.

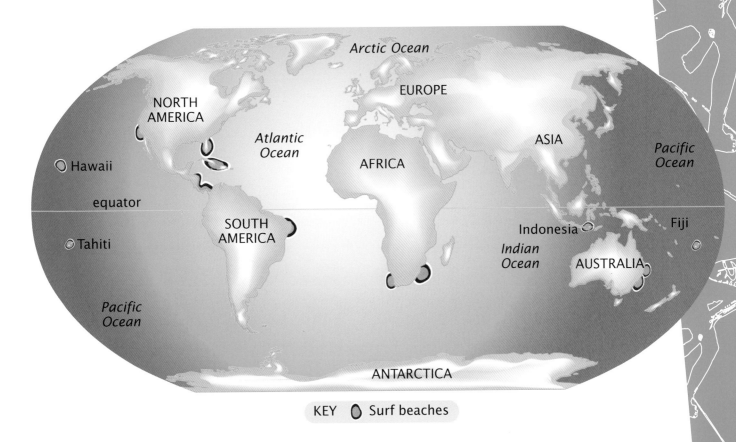

Arctic Ocean

EUROPE

NORTH AMERICA

Atlantic Ocean

ASIA

Pacific Ocean

Hawaii

AFRICA

equator

SOUTH AMERICA

Tahiti

Indonesia

Fiji

Indian Ocean

AUSTRALIA

Pacific Ocean

ANTARCTICA

KEY ◗ Surf beaches

WOMEN AND SURFING

Women have been part of the surfing scene in Hawaii and California since the early 1920s, but it was in the late 1950s and early 1960s with the release of films with a surfing theme that the sport became popular with women. In the film *Gidget Goes Hawaiian*, Linda Benson did some surfing sequences. She later won the Pacific Coast Women's Surf Championship in 1959, 1960 and 1961.

The first all-female professional competition, the Hang Ten Championships, began in 1975 in Malibu, California, and was won by Margo Godfrey. In the 1970s, Margo Godfrey was the best woman surfer in the world.

Today, the women's surfing tour is run by the ASP.

ACTION FACT

One of the first women to ride on a surfboard was Isabel Letham, who rode with Duke Kahanomoku when the Duke demonstrated surfboarding to Australians in 1915.

Jacqueline Silva from Brazil competing in Oahu, Hawaii, in 2001.

SURFING
CHAMPIONS

Surfing is a popular pastime for the general public at beaches during the summer, but top male and female surfers practice and compete all year round.

Top surfers come from many countries around the world. Currently the male and female surf champions come from the home of surfing, Hawaii, and from other places in the United States and Australia. World-class competitions for both men and women are held on beaches around the world each year.

↗ Layne Beachley

- Born May 24, 1972
- Lives in Dee Why, New South Wales, Australia
- Has been competing for 12 years

Career highlights

- 22 wins in World Championship events
- World Champion female surfer in 1998, 1999, 2000 and 2001

↗ Melanie Redman-Carr

- Born July 4, 1975
- Lives in Dunsborough, Western Australia

Career highlights

- Winner of Billabong Girls' event in Hawaii in 1998
- Three competition wins in 1999
- Ranked number two female World Champion surfer in 2001

↗ Keala Kennelly

- Born August 13, 1978
- Lives in Kauai, Hawaii

Career highlights

- Eight wins in World Championship events
- In Tahiti, secured a perfect 10 point score with a tube ride in 2001
- Ranked fifth in the world in 2001–2002

↗ Sunny Garcia

- Born January 14, 1970
- Lives in Kauai, Hawaii
- Has been one of the world's top surfers for the past 15 years
- Has won 35 championship surfing competitions

Career highlights

- Won seven surfing competitions in Australia and in the United States in 2000
- Became the ASP World Champion surfer in 2000
- A video game, "Sunny Garcia Surfing," became available in 2002

↗ C.J. Hobgood

- Born June 7, 1979
- Lives in Florida

Career highlights

- Has won three championship surfing competitions
- Became the ASP World Champion surfer in 2001

↗ Mark Occhilupo

- Born June 16, 1968
- Lives in Queensland, Australia

Career highlights

- Had 20 wins in championship surfing competitions, 1983–2000
- Became the ASP World Champion surfer in 1999

↗ Kelly Slater

- Born February 11, 1972
- Lives in Florida
- Considered to be the best surfer of all time
- Has won 21 surfing competitions

Career highlights

- World Champion six times
- In 1992 at age 20, became the youngest ASP World Champion surfer
- Winner of the Quicksilver event in Hawaii in 2002

THEN AND NOW

1907	1912	1915	1920s	1928	1930s	1932
Surfboard riding began in the United States after a demonstration of the sport in California by George Freeth of Hawaii.	Australian C.D. Paterson brought a surfboard home from Hawaii, but no one in Australia could ride it.	Duke Kahanamoku, Olympic medal-winning swimmer and surfer from Hawaii, demonstrated how to ride a surfboard in Sydney, Australia.	Surfing increased in popularity in Hawaii and Southern California. Tom Blake designed and built lighter surfboards weighing a third less than older-style boards.	The first Pacific Coast Surfboard Championships took place.	The first mass-produced surfboards, constructed of balsa and redwood and laminated together with a waterproof glue, were sold in the United States.	Tom Blake took out the first patent on a surfboard. A fin was added to the bottom of Tom Blake surfboards to assist balance in 1935.

1920s

1946	1960s	1966	1969	1979	1981	1990s	2002
The first fiberglass surfboard was built by Preston "Pete" Peterson.	Hollywood surfing movies, music and fashion helped to increase the popularity of surfing.	Australian champion Nat Young began the trend toward shorter surfboards.	Mike Doyle became the first surfer to win a cash prize in a surfing competition.	Mark Richards of Newcastle, Australia, with two fins on his board, won the Championship. He also won in 1980, 1981 and 1982.	Simon Anderson from Sydney developed a tri-fin board (a surfboard with three fins).	Surfing magazines, video games and the Internet kept surfers informed about their sport.	Six-time World Champion, Kelly Slater, returned to professional competition after a three-year break. An Australian company produced bamboo surfboards with a recyclable foam core.

1960s

1990s

FREE WORLD CHAMP POSTER • WIN MICK FANNING'S BOARD

Surfing

TRANSWORLD SURF
PIONEERING THE NEXT FRONTIER

EXCLUSIVE
SUPER

WAVES
surfGIRL
THE SURFING MAG WITH THE GIRL'S EYE VIEW

Riptide

BEAT THE CHILL!
THE ULTIMATE WINTER SURVIVAL KIT:
PRO TIPS; WETSUIT GUIDE;
HOT WINTER WEAR; AND MORE...

EXCLUSIVE
JACK JOHNSON
INTERVIEW!
CHELSEA GEORGESON CHATS
TO THE MAN OF YOUR DREAMS P.78

GENERATION
NEXT

RELATED ACTION SPORTS

Wakeboarding

Wakeboarders ride attached to a short board by footstraps. They are towed behind a motor boat at about 19 miles (30 kilometers) per hour. The sport is a cross between surfing and water-skiing. The wakeboarder launches off the **wake** of the boat and takes off into the air. Once in the air the wakeboarder performs a variety of aerial tricks and maneuvers over fun boxes, similar to skateboarding ramps, which have been placed in the water.

In competition, a panel of four judges rides in the boat and gives the wakeboarder scores for each trick. Wakeboarding began in 1985 and has become a part of the Gravity Games and the Summer X Games. In the 1990s, the World Wakeboard Association was formed to help develop the sport worldwide.

↗ Wakeboarding is the fastest-growing water sport in the world.

Boardsailing

Boardsailing is also known as sailboarding. The rider is on a small, light board with a sail attached. There are racing events including slalom races where sailboarders race to and around markers. Freestyle events have the riders performing aerial stunts high above the water.

↗ Boardsailing was introduced as an Olympic event for men in 1984 and for women in 1992.

GLOSSARY

aerial a maneuver where the surfer flies into the air off the wave and becomes airborne

boogie board a surfboard used for bodyboarding

drop in to take off on a wave

fiberglass woven glass cloth that, when saturated with resin, provides the protective outer coating of a surfboard

plane to ride on the surface of the water

polyester a synthetic substance used to make resins, plastics and fibers

polystyrene a plastic foam used to make the center of a surfboard

polyurethane a rigid, synthetic substance used to make the center of a surfboard

resin a liquid plastic substance which acts as the glue that binds the surfboard together

shorebreak surf breaking close to the beach

velcro tape with two strips of fabric that hook together

wake the trail left in the water behind a boat

wax a substance applied to a surfboard to make it less slippery

wipe-out to fall or to get knocked off the surfboard

INDEX